D0671546

Earn. Save. Give.

Devotional Readings for Home

Earn. Save. Give.
Wesley's Simple Rules for Money

Earn. Save. Give.
978-1-63088-392-8
978-1-63088-393-5 eBook

Earn. Save. Give. - Large Print Edition
978-1-63088-394-2

Earn. Save. Give. - Leader Guide
978-1-63088-395-9
978-1-63088-396-6 eBook

Earn. Save. Give. - DVD
978-1-63088-397-3

Earn. Save. Give. - Program Guide
978-1-63088-398-0 Flash Drive
978-1-63088-399-7 Download

Earn. Save. Give. - Youth Study Book
978-1-63088-400-0
978-1-63088-401-7 eBook

Earn. Save. Give. - Children's Leader Guide
978-1-63088-402-4

Earn. Save. Give. - Devotional Readings for Home
978-1-5018-0507-3
978-1-5018-0509-7 Package of 25
978-1-5018-0508-0 eBook

For more information, visit www.AbingdonPress.com.

Also by James A. Harnish

A Disciple's Heart

A Disciple's Path

Believe in Me

Converge Bible Studies: Women of the Bible

Journey to the Center of the Faith

Living with the Mind of Christ

Passion, Power, and Praise

Radical Renovation

reConnect

Rejoicing in Hope

Simple Rules for Money

Strength for the Broken Places

You Only Have to Die

JAMES A. HARNISH

EARN. SAVE. GIVE.

Wesley's Simple Rules for Money

DEVOTIONAL READINGS FOR HOME
by Frank Ramirez

Abingdon Press / *Nashville*

Earn. Save. Give.
Wesley's Simple Rules for Money

Devotional Readings for Home
by Frank Ramirez

Copyright © 2015 by Abingdon Press
All rights reserved.

No part of this work may be reproduced or transmitted in any form or by any means, electronic or mechanical, including photocopying and recording, or by any information storage or retrieval system, except as may be expressly permitted by the 1976 Copyright Act or in writing from the publisher. Requests for permission can be addressed to Permissions, The United Methodist Publishing House, P.O. Box 280988, 2222 Rosa L. Parks Boulevard, Nashville, TN 37228-0988, or e-mailed to permissions@umpublishing.org.

This book is printed on elemental, chlorine-free paper.
ISBN 978-1-5018-0507-3

Scripture quotations unless noted otherwise are from the Common English Bible. Copyright © 2011 by the Common English Bible. All rights reserved. Used by permission. www.CommonEnglishBible.com.

Scripture quotation marked KJV is from The Authorized (King James) Version. Rights in the Authorized Version in the United Kingdom are vested in the Crown. Reproduced by permission of the Crown's patentee, Cambridge University Press.

Scripture quotations marked NRSV are taken from the New Revised Standard Version of the Bible, copyright 1989, Division of Christian Education of the National Council of the Churches of Christ in the United States of America. Used by permission. All rights reserved.

15 16 17 18 19 20 21 22 23 24 — 10 9 8 7 6 5 4 3 2 1
MANUFACTURED IN THE UNITED STATES OF AMERICA

CONTENTS

INTRODUCTION

One year during the Super Bowl broadcast, a soft drink company aired a commercial pretending to show the origins of halftime. Two old-time football teams wearily lined up for the next play, wearing very little padding beyond their leather helmets, when a bevy of twenties-style flappers drove up in a roadster. Holding up bottles of soft drink, the flappers asked the players to take a break. Soon everyone was guzzling a soft drink, snapping selfies with a box camera, and generally having a fine time.

In the minds of many Christians, the offering is not worship; it's a break in the action. Only when halftime is over does worship resume. And why shouldn't they get that impression, when the offering consists of a desultory reading, a lifeless prayer, a tepid instrumental, and the singing of a well-worn stanza?

But in the Hebrew Scriptures, worship is centered in the offering! It's not a sideshow; it's *the* show. And in the New Testament, one of the high points of Holy Week is when a widow makes an offering in which she, like Jesus on the cross, gives all that she has.

Money is not a dirty word. John Wesley, Christian theologian, evangelist, and founder of Methodism, certainly didn't think so. In his sermon, "The Use of Money," Wesley preached that it is the "love of money," not the money itself, that lies at "the root of all evil." [1]

Earn. Save. Give.: Wesley's Simple Rules for Money, by author and pastor James A. Harnish, is the basis for a four-week stewardship program that includes videos, a small group study, lessons for children and youth, sermon starters, worship resources, a program guide, and this daily devotional.

The program will show how, in the words of Wesley, to earn all you can, save all you can, and give all you can. In this devotional, we will learn each week about Wesley and his advice regarding money; then I will tell stories ancient and modern to muse about what we have learned and to show that it's doable!

The offering is not halftime; it's at the very center of worship. We might even say it's the high point of Sabbath, when we cease to be spectators and commit to participating in the ongoing ministry of Jesus.

WE DON'T NEED MORE MONEY; WE NEED WISDOM

Happy are those who find wisdom
  and those who gain understanding.
Her profit is better than silver,
  and her gain better than gold.
                    (Proverbs 3:13-14)

The eighteenth century was a time of major social and economic change in England. The economic inequality between the comfortable, affluent aristocracy and the beleaguered, poverty-stricken lower classes was growing larger and more tenuous.

The first Methodists came on the scene with a life-giving proclamation of the gospel that offered hope for transformation in every area of human experience. Some historians say that the Methodist revival saved

England from the kind of violent revolution that swept across Western Europe.[1] The personal and spiritual disciplines that John Wesley practiced and taught enabled people in the lower classes to become more responsible, better educated, and more prosperous. Soon Wesley faced the unexpected predicament of Methodist people accumulating wealth, wearing fine clothing, and building more attractive homes and preaching houses.

Wesley responded to this change of economic circumstances in his classic sermon, "The Use of Money." He used the defining word from the Proverbs when he declared that "the right use of money" is "an excellent branch of Christian wisdom." In fact, the word *wisdom* appears seven times in this sermon. He acknowledged that money was "a subject largely spoken of . . . by men of the world; but not sufficiently considered by those whom God hath chosen out of the world." [2]

We could say the same thing about many congregations today in which the only time money is mentioned is during an annual pledge drive to support the church budget. But Wesley's concern in the sermon was not to raise money for the Methodist movement; his purpose was to equip Methodists to manage and use their money in the most faithful and effective ways. In this sermon, he set out the essential themes that he continued to proclaim in multiple sermons that were intended to provide wisdom on both the spiritual and practical aspects of managing money.

From that starting point, Mr. Wesley outlined what he called "three plain rules" on the use of money. They are as simple, clear, and memorable as any of the Old Testament proverbs:

- Gain all you can.
- Save all you can.
- Give all you can.

For this study, we have replaced the word *gain* with *earn*, to make Wesley's rules more directly applicable to our times.

"The Use of Money" laid out a description of what it means to live by those rules, and he reaffirmed them in a number of his other sermons. Two-and-a-half centuries later, Wesley's rules continue to provide practical and positive wisdom for discovering a faithful, biblical, and hopeful approach to our financial lives.

-From *Earn. Save. Give.*, by James A. Harnish

1. Ancient and Awesome

Honor the LORD with your wealth
and with the first of all your crops.
Then your barns will be filled with plenty,
and your vats will burst with wine.
                                    (Proverbs 3:9-10)

I was a first-year seminary student almost forty years ago, with only a few weeks of New Testament Greek under my belt, when a professor offered an advanced-level course that sounded intriguing. He intended to examine and explore ancient letters written by ordinary Christians during the era when our faith was illegal. These ancient letters concerned everyday matters such lost cloaks, travel arrangements, complaints about kids, the weather—and money!

I was eager to take the course, but the professor said I would only be accepted if I passed a test showing that I could read as much Greek as students who had mastered a full year's study. The task seemed impossible, but I studied hard, took the test, and passed. Smoke and mirrors? Or maybe prayer really works!

The course was great fun. I learned about ordinary life in the ancient world. One letter that I translated survived only in tattered fragments of papyrus. An early Christian wrote from Rome to Alexandria,

Egypt, but not about church. The letter was all about grain and barley shipments, the baking of loaves, and the transport of cloth. It seems likely that the letter writer took part in the vital trade that kept the populations of large cities such as Rome alive, while making an honest profit to support his Christian community. The addressee of the letter was told "to deliver the money to...Maximus the Papas, and get a receipt from him. But the profits [from the bread and the cloth] are to be trusted to Theonas. I want to find it in my account when I arrive in Alexandria."[3]

Maximus was the *papas* (the "pope" or bishop) of Alexandria from A.D. 264 to 282. Theonas would later succeed Maximus in the same office after his death.[4]

Notice that this letter was not about theology, but money. The early church in the Roman Empire was built after the model of the Roman household, which existed for the economic protection and support of all its members. Before most believers became Christians, they would have taken part in their family's craft or business and prayed to the family's god. After baptism, the believers would no longer pray to that god; they would become a new family that prayed together to Jesus.

The point is that from the beginning, Christian churches have served not only as spiritual outposts but also as economic units. Wisdom in earning, saving, and giving money has allowed Christians to look after each other. These activities are part of our roots as the church.

Though some people think of the church's world as separate from the "real" world of finance and economics, the first Christians did not separate financial accountability from their call to be faithful disciples. Neither should we.

Divine Wisdom, Giver of all good things, grant us a share of your wisdom as we seek to witness in all we sing, pray, praise, and spend. Amen.

2. I Have a Name

> *"Listen to this! A farmer went out to scatter seed." (Mark 4:3)*

The parable of the sower, found in the Gospels of Matthew, Mark, and Luke, is no exercise in gardening. When the farmer goes out to his field to sow, it is an act that could mean life or death for his family. Their economic well-being depends on how well he does his job.

In this parable, Jesus tells how the seed falls on various kinds of soil and in some cases fails altogether. However, the parable concludes, "Other seed fell into good soil and brought forth grain, growing up and increasing and yielding thirty and sixty and a hundredfold" (Mark 4:8 NRSV).

Jesus went on to explain how the word of God can be planted in different people. In some it will wither and fail, while in others it will bring forth great fruit. Perhaps one reason the parable is so well remembered is that that's what life is like for so many people.

I knew a denominational official who had worked many years in African missions and had returned to America to make films. He watched an African man sowing seeds in a primitive but effective manner, and he asked the man for permission to film him sowing, because it would make a great backdrop for a reading of this Scripture.

The purpose of the film was to encourage greater giving to mission projects, and this graphic illustration of the text did indeed have an effect on giving. It was like the seed that the farmer sowed on good soil, bearing much fruit.

The African man consented to be filmed, but afterward he came up to the filmmaker and asked for a moment of his time. The filmmaker assumed the sower was going to ask for payment, but he didn't. He simply asked, "Don't you want to know my name?"

The story was a reminder to all of us that our economic choices are not just theoretical, numerical, or financial. They are tied to real people with real lives, who have names and who matter to God. Our economic choices include looking for the best bargains to provide for ourselves and our families, but they also must bear witness to our Savior, and they cannot bring harm to others.

We ought to know the names of our brothers and sisters who make our clothes, grow our food, and build our cars, whether five miles away or five thousand. Once someone has a name, we are more likely to make wise choices in the ways we spend our money.

God whose name is I AM, we are together around this great globe and are your servants. As we name you Lord, bless us that we may name each other as brother and sister in one family, one economy, one in love and service. Amen.

3. Daily Bread

> *I know the experience of being in need and of*
> *having more than enough; I have learned the*
> *secret to being content in any and every cir-*
> *cumstance, whether full or hungry or whether*
> *having plenty or being poor. I can endure*
> *all these things through the power of the one*
> *who gives me strength. (Philippians 4:12-13)*

A *mashal* is a term used in the Book of Proverbs for a saying that is self-evident, that means what it says. In the thirtieth chapter of Proverbs we meet a sage named Agur who uses a mashal to make an important point about wisdom and economics.

Everything about Agur is mysterious. His name and lineage suggest he might be a foreign-born official who had important religious duties in Israel. He is a masterful poet, a perceptive observer of human nature, and he offers a prayer that is striking because it encapsulates the contentment most of us ought to seek in having enough but not too much.[5]

Two things I ask of you;
    don't keep them from me before I die:
Fraud and lies—
    keep far from me!

> Don't give me either poverty or wealth;
>> give me just the food I need.
>> Or I'll be full and deny you,
>> and say, "Who is the Lord?"
>> Or I'll be poor and steal,
>> and dishonor my God's name.
>>> (Proverbs 30:7-9)

It's impossible to say if Agur's prayer had any influence on Jesus when he taught the Lord's Prayer to his disciples, but one can make the argument that our daily bread is one of the factors that leads us away from temptation. That's certainly why Agur wisely asks to be delivered from poverty, because otherwise he might dishonor God by stealing. Agur realizes that riches, the other extreme, can also be a trap, because if he is too satisfied he will no longer recognize God as Father. By asking, "Who is the Lord?" he will be dishonoring the holiness of God's name.

Our culture is telling us that having enough is not enough. We need more. The result is that many of us believe we never have enough, even if we achieve more success than we ever dreamed possible. The way of the world is a fraud and a lie. If our choices about money are taken out of the realm of faith and wrestled with only in a worldly setting, we will never find the place Agur points to, neither very rich nor very poor.

Agur's mashal is succinct and memorable. It is wisdom at its best.

Lord God of all days and all seasons, may we never forget you, whether rich or poor, in prosperity or adversity. You are with us always, even unto the end of the age! Amen.

4. Borders Between Rich and Poor

> *"The Spirit of the Lord is upon me,*
>   *because the Lord has anointed me.*
> *He has sent me to preach good news to the*
> *poor...." (Luke 4:18)*

The sight of earth from space is so vivid and complex that some of the early astronauts asked for books of paint samples so they would have a vocabulary adequate to describe the colors they saw! But one thing astronauts could not see from space was the Great Wall of China. That's an urban myth. Or is it an orbital myth? The Great Wall cannot be seen from space.[6]

Surprisingly, however, there is something that can be seen clearly from space: the border between rich countries and poor countries. Politics and economics are visible from space. You can see where the money is, and where it ends.

At least that's what former astronaut John Grunsfeld reported. "Wealthy countries are lined in green and then you see the country next door that has no water," he said at a meeting of the American Astronomical Society. Grunsfeld, who made five space flights and visited the Hubble Space Telescope three times to improve the visibility of things millions of light years away, took time to look down on Earth from his vantage point three hundred miles into space. During the fourteen years when his flights were taken, he saw the gap between rich and poor countries widen. Rich countries became greener. Poor countries grew browner as they became more arid. More forests were cleared. More rivers were dammed. The poor countries had fewer trees. "It's really very disturbing," he said.[7]

When Jesus visited his hometown synagogue, he quoted from Isaiah that he had come to preach good news to the poor. Part of that passage was "to proclaim the year of the Lord's favor" (4:19), a year of debt relief known as the Jubilee. Jesus' teaching was damaging to his popularity.

When we preach the economic wisdom of the New Testament today, our poll numbers go down as well. But when we can look down from space and clearly see the disparity between rich and poor, doesn't it tell us that the wise use of our money includes bridging the economic gap both at home and around the world?

God whose creation, viewed from space, fills us with awe and challenges us to share more, make me an instrument of your peace. Amen.

5. What If?

> *But anyone who needs wisdom should ask*
> *God, whose very nature is to give to everyone*
> *without a second thought, without keeping*
> *score. Wisdom will certainly be given to those*
> *who ask. (James 1:5)*

Have you ever asked yourself, "What would I do if someone gave me a million dollars?" Answers tend to vary, from spending it all madly to saving it for the future, or giving it away to friends, family, and favorite charities, including one's church.

For most of us it's a game. But one day an old man with a trace of a German accent walked into the church office of a Mennonite pastor, took a seat, and asked him, "What would your congregation do if you had access to two million dollars?"

Perhaps something in the old man's bearing told the pastor that this was no theoretical question. The man went on to tell the pastor that he had been a soldier in the German army during World War II, fighting during the terrible winter on the Russian front. He developed typhoid fever and soon was gravely ill. Finally he was nursed back to health by a Russian Mennonite woman who had been forced to work in the German army hospital.

Afterward, at great personal risk to herself and despite the fact that they were enemies in the conflict, the Russian Mennonite woman saved his life by providing papers that sent him home instead of back to the front.

After the war, the man started a new life in America, worked hard, and grew rich. He tried to track down the woman who had helped him, but he was unable to find any trace of her. He decided in her memory to make a gift to a Mennonite congregation in America, and he had selected that pastor's congregation from the phone book.

What did the church do with two million dollars? They formed a committee so the money would be used wisely. They decided to support several different ministries, such as Habitat for Humanity, overseas service projects, grants for youth attending Christian colleges, disaster response programs, and many others. A great deal of thought and wisdom went into the preservation and use of the funds. The challenge to be good stewards led to good plans, so the gift would neither be wasted, as in the parable of the prodigal son (Luke 15:11-32), nor buried, as in the parable of the valuable coins (Matthew 25:14-30).[8]

What would you have done? How would your church have handled the gift? Perhaps your congregation already has a procedure for handling large gifts. How many people are involved in the decision-making process? How successful is the procedure? Maybe you don't have a plan at all. Are you assuming you won't get large gifts? Have large gifts in the past been spent, then disappeared?

As a church, prepare for gifts. Think about it. Plan for them.

God of life, whether I'm dealing with amounts great or small, I count on you to direct me in gaining, saving, and giving. Amen.

WEEK ONE
ACTIVITIES

Individual

- Pick a page of Proverbs in your Bible at random and highlight any proverbs about money.
- Put a change jar at your school or workplace. Designate a charity for the change you collect.
- Write an acrostic poem for the word *wisdom* about money.
- Review your pattern of giving. How regular is it?
- Pray the Prayer of Agur. (See the Prayer Pages at the end.)
- Consult a Bible dictionary or the Internet for insights on giving, offerings, and sacrifice in the Bible.
- Look up and read John Wesley's sermon, "The Use of Money."
- Estimate how many books are in your home. How many books do you have about money?
- Count how many times money is mentioned in an hour of worship. Compare with the number of times money is mentioned on a sports show or prime-time television.

Family

- Dream about what you would do for the church with $2 million.
- Create two digital or physical collages representing needs and resources in the world. Talk about ways to bring the two together.
- Do a computer search for folk tales about the wise use of money. Illustrate with crayons.
- Design new money. Whose face would be displayed? Add a motto from Proverbs.

EARN. SAVE. GIVE.

—WEEK TWO—

EARN ALL YOU CAN

Laziness brings poverty;
hard work makes one rich.
(Proverbs 10:4)

When was the last time you were surprised by what the preacher had to say?

I'll never forget an old guy in the first congregation I served who had been in the church all of his life. He sat in the back row and went to sleep during the sermon every Sunday morning. One day on the way out of worship he explained his behavior. "Well, Preacher," he said, "I listen to the first part of your sermon and when I know I can trust what you're going to say, I figure I can get in a good nap." It became my personal challenge to surprise that guy with something he didn't expect just to keep him awake.

I suspect that many of John Wesley's most faithful followers were a lot like those of us who listen to sermons every Sunday morning. We may not go to

25

sleep, but once we hear the Scripture and listen to the opening illustration, we often assume that we know what the preacher is going to say. The challenge for the preacher is to surprise us with something we didn't expect to hear.

John Wesley's sermon "The Use of Money" must have come as a surprise to some of the early Methodists. It still has the power to take us by surprise.

The surprise came when Wesley contradicted the assumption that wealth and money are inherently evil. Instead, Wesley called money "an excellent gift of God." Wesley raised the bar on the spiritual importance of money when he called it "a most compendious instrument of transacting all manner of business, and (if we use it according to Christian wisdom) of doing all manner of good."[1]

Wesley declared "the right use of money" to be "an excellent branch of Christian wisdom" that is "not sufficiently considered by those whom God hath chosen out of the world. . . . Neither do they understand how to employ it to the greatest advantage."[2]

Wesley's critique of Christians who do not know how to manage or use money "to the greatest advantage" could still apply to many faithful people and congregations today. I've known people who believed that wise financial planning was somehow a contradiction of their trust in God. I've known congregations that functioned without wise management of their resources and without adequate methods of financial accountability. Regardless of the sincerity of their faith, sooner or later those individuals and congregations always end up in some kind of financial crisis.

By contrast, I've been grateful for the wise, experienced, and deeply faithful laypersons in every congregation I've served who use their best knowledge and experience with money to guide the church in the wise stewardship of the gifts of God's people. Their financial wisdom is not a contradiction of their faith, but an expression of it.

-From *Earn. Save. Give.*, by James A. Harnish

6. Earn While the Earning Is Good

Because the LORD your God is bringing you into a wonderful land, . . . a land where you will eat food without any shortage—you won't lack a thing there."
(Deuteronomy 8:7-9)

In 1724, the German-born Christopher Sauer (1695–1758) came as an immigrant to the New World.

Soon after his arrival in Germantown, Pennsylvania, not far from Philadelphia, he wrote back to friends in Germany.

After describing the difficulties of the voyage, he enthused about the many wonders and opportunities in the New World, and especially the freedom from European ways: "Now we are here in a well-blessed land.... The spirit of this world promises her admirers a great fortune weekly. When a day laborer or artisan arrives here without debts, he can then buy property in two or three years of one hundred acres of fields, and forests, with wheat, trees, and other gardens, as well as a soundly built stone house. This is more independent than a nobleman's estate in Germany."[3]

Sauer could not believe the manner in which he, an immigrant, could live in his new country. "I live in a house where I have a large room...a kitchen, attic, garden, cellar, stable, a cow and two pigs, as well as a large orchard with thirty-six apple trees, many peaches and cherries. When the cow and the pigs are fattened from the peaches and apples, I hope to have fifty measures of apples left to shake down. I also have free split firewood on the farm."[4]

Sauer began working to advance himself. He had been a tailor in the Old World but soon demonstrated his mechanical genius as an inventor by teaching himself twenty-six trades, including joiner, pharmacist, botanist, apothecary, surgeon, clockmaker, lathe operator, glazier, lampblack manufacturer, and most of all printer. He taught himself the skills of bookbinding and editing, along with the drawing of lead and wire. He made all his own printing tools and ink, and he even operated his own paper mill. Soon things were going so well that, as he noted, "my wife is getting very fat."

His started his own press. Sauer printed hymnals, books, and pamphlets for people of all faiths as well as German-language newspapers and almanacs. In 1743, he printed the first Bible in America that was written in a European language, in this case German.

It was his industry and his desire to earn all he could that made it possible for Christopher Sauer to save all he could and then later, as a philanthropist, to give all he could to charitable causes: aiding immigrants, fighting slavery, and working for the rights of Native Americans.

Save all you can. Give all you can. Yes, but first earn all you can!

God, the source of all good things, grant that I might use my time wisely, honoring you in earning according to your good will. Amen.

7. If Only

> *Riches gotten quickly will dwindle,*
> *but those who acquire them gradually*
> *become wealthy.*
>
> *(Proverbs 13:11)*

Have you ever found yourself wishing for a bolt from the blue, something so improbably lucky that you'd be set up for life! Especially without working for it?

If only this time you'd win the lottery! If only there were a coin, or a piece of furniture, or an old book that you would discover in your home that was worth far more than you ever imagined! If only, while digging around in the back yard, you came across something more valuable than your wildest dreams!

One reason people dream of things like this is because every now and then it actually happens. Never mind all those depressing statistics about how quickly overnight millionaires go bankrupt. Why can't money just fall into our laps?

Which leads me to a California couple, whom we will call John and Mary, who noticed something odd sticking out of the ground in their yard.

It was an old can. They dug it up. Then they found another. And another. There were eight cans filled with nineteenth-century gold coins. Real gold coins.

Real, rare gold coins. Later, John said, "I thought any second an old miner with a mule was going to appear."

The couple contacted a firm that specialized in American coins, and the firm quickly confirmed that the eight cans were filled with over 1,400 authentic, well-preserved US coins dated between 1847 and 1894. The coins were worth over ten million dollars!

According to a report by Ruben Vives in the Los Angeles Times, the couple "said they plan to keep some of the coins and sell others . . . with the intention of donating part of the proceeds to charity." Some of the rest would be used to pay off their home.

Mary was quoted as saying, "Whatever answers you seek, they might be right at home. The answer to our difficulties was there under our feet for years." [5]

It's a wonderful story—so why don't all of us start digging in our backyards? Of course, it's because this kind of thing almost never happens.

As fun as it might be to dream, today's Scripture from Proverbs reminds us that when it comes to earning all we can, nothing is more certain to produce riches than hard work.

God who bestows daily blessings, bless me and mine with the ability and opportunity to work, to save, and to give. Amen.

8. Just Like Ferris, Sort Of

> *"One by one, the manager sent for each*
> *person who owed his master money. He*
> *said to the first, 'How much do you owe my*
> *master?' He said, 'Nine hundred gallons of*
> *olive oil.' The manager said to him, 'Take*
> *your contract, sit down quickly, and write*
> *four hundred fifty gallons.'"(Luke 16:5-6)*

There's a scene in the movie *Ferris Bueller's Day Off* that reminds me of Jesus' parable about an unjust steward. In the film Ferris, a high school senior, is faking an illness so he can take a day off from school. The principal, who despises Ferris, calls his mother to let her know that her son has missed school so often that he may not graduate.

Mom protests that her son has not missed nearly that many days. The principal is gleefully prepared to give her a cold dose of reality when, as he watches, the number of Bueller's absences displayed on the computer shrinks before his eyes. Meanwhile all of us watching the movie realize that Ferris has hacked into the school's database through his home computer.[6]

Like the unjust steward, who faces expulsion from his master's service for having cut corners, and who adjusts the accounts of his master's creditors and changes reality, Ferris lowers the number of days he's been absent. As with the parable, we know that what we're seeing is wrong, and yet we end up cheering the roguish hero.

Throughout the film, Ferris charms everyone and always lands on his feet. As the school secretary tells the principal, everyone loves Ferris: "They think he's a righteous dude." Similarly, the unjust steward who has hacked into his master's accounts has earned the gratitude of his master's debtors.

Before you condemn the unjust steward, consider this: the economic system in Jesus' time made it difficult for poor farmers to succeed. They knew what it was like to fall into spiraling debt, never to recover. Many were offered cheap credit on their family farms but were unable to keep up the payments and lost their land. That's one reason why day laborers appear so often in the parables. When Jesus told the story, these people may have found themselves cheering for what was done, even if it was dishonest.

Jesus concluded the parable by challenging those of us who consider ourselves "children of light" to treat each other as well as those who seem less than honest appear to do. But we don't have to cut corners, hack into computers, or change reality in order to earn all we can. We can do it the way that's honest and long lasting—through ambition, attitude, and action.

And while we're at it, we ought to be careful not to fall deeply into debt. We might cheer for Ferris Bueller, but we don't have to be him!

Lord, grant me wisdom and patience as I seek to be responsible in all things. Amen.

9. Dropping A Hint

> *"Look, I'm sending you as sheep among wolves. Therefore, be wise as snakes and innocent as doves." (Matthew 10:16)*

Before Hurricane Katrina struck in 2005, Hurricane Camille in 1969 was considered the benchmark against which all other hurricanes were measured. After Camille devastated portions of Mississippi and Louisiana, government agencies and church organizations sent disaster relief teams. They worked together to alleviate the suffering of the survivors.

There are occasions, however, when sacred and secular folks, all of them working very hard, will see the same situation in a different light. One group of eleven church workers thought the dilapidated homes that had been completely destroyed by Hurricane

Camille ought to be replaced with more modern conveniences. Specifically, many of the homes, owned by the poorest of the poor, had no indoor plumbing. The eleven workers thought it would take little or no extra effort to upgrade the homes they were restoring.

The government policy, however, insisted the workers were only to build to "pre-disaster conditions." The volunteers complained that this was "poor stewardship." The added cost of improvements was negligible and would raise the standard of living for these very poor people who had lost everything. Nevertheless, the workers were told there would be no authorization to add indoor plumbing for homes with outhouses, and that was that.

What would you do? What did they do? One of the workers devised a special plan. He purchased an old toilet and a piece of plumbing pipe with his own money. Then, when the crew arrived at a new work site, he threw the two items into the wreckage.

Government inspectors (who, after all, were just doing their jobs) would arrive on the scene, see the toilet and pipe, and assumed these had been part of the home before the storm. The disaster relief work crew, saying nothing about the old toilet, let the inspectors draw their own conclusions. The funds to build a bathroom at the work site were always approved.

When the supervisor from church headquarters arrived, he learned what had been done and decided in the end to say nothing.[7]

Dishonesty? Good stewardship? I look on this example as one of the more imaginative ways of creating value I've ever heard of. It certainly succeeded in "earning" funds for home improvement.

What would you have done?

We thank you then, Creator,
For all things bright and good,
The seed-time and the harvest,
Our life, our health, our food.
Accept the gifts we offer,
For all your love imparts,
And what you most would welcome,
Our humble, thankful hearts.[8]

10. Favorite Founder

Laziness brings poverty;
hard work makes one rich.
(Proverbs 10:4)

Everyone has a favorite Founding Father or Mother—at least I do. And the favorite can change depending on my mood and the day of the week. John Adams, Alexander Hamilton, Abigail Adams— I continue to be impressed and inspired by all they did to improve our nation and our world.

But I keep coming back to Benjamin Franklin (1706–1790).

Yes, Franklin was a genius in every sense. He had a way with words, as we see from the wise, clever sayings he wrote in *Poor Richard's Almanac*, such as "The Lord helps those who help themselves." The sayings were so filled with truth that many people assume they came from the Bible.

He was a printer and so was able to get his homespun wisdom out to the public.

He founded the first fire department, the first public library, and an anti-slavery society.

He was a scientist, and, unlike the work of many predecessors that was only appreciated by the deepest thinkers, his inventions—such as the lightning rod, the Franklin stove, and bifocals—directly and profoundly changed the lives of ordinary people.

As a politician and a diplomat, he was the most admired American in Europe.

All these things were possible because Franklin set about making himself independent by earning all he could. He demonstrated that America was a place where poor people could become rich.

This was hardly possible in other countries, where for the most part people did not become rich; they were born rich. In America, by way of contrast, it was possible for anyone who had ambition and skill to "earn all you can."

Think of some of the popular sayings about money which are attributed to Benjamin Franklin.

> A penny saved is a penny earned.
> Rather go to bed without dinner than to rise in debt.
> An investment in knowledge always pays the best interest.
> If you want to become rich, never waste your time or money.
> Wealth mainly depends on two things: hard work and moderation.
> Remember that money can multiply itself.

Come to think of it, today's proverb, shown at the top of this devotion, sounds like it could hve been written by Benjamin Franklin! Surely John Wesley would have approved.

Lord, grant that I might, according to your will, earn all I can, save all I can, and give all I can. Amen.

WEEK TWO
ACTIVITIES

Individual

- Dream up a fundraiser never before used by your church.
- Before sharing your earnings, pick a favorite charity and research how the money is used.
- Write an acrostic poem for *earn* about what your earnings can mean for the church.
- Discuss what church program or church project you are most excited about.
- Think about the way you earn money. How is God honored in that process?
- Pray the Lord's Prayer. (See the Prayer Pages at the end of this book.)
- Calculate and exceed the percentage of your budgeted weekly offering to the church.
- Chart the actual percentage and amount of your offering week by week.
- Check out and read a book from your public library or church library on the subject of Christian earning.

Family

- Place a cup in the middle of the table. Encourage each family member to give twenty-five cents per person per meal, which will be donated at the end of the week to the church or a favorite charity.

- Pray the Prayer of King David together. (See the Prayer Pages at the end of this book.)
- Play a board game involving money. Discuss how kind or cruel the game is.
- Write a script or draw a storyboard for a public service announcement regarding the benefits of earning, saving, and giving.
- Sing "All Good Gifts (We Plow the Fields and Scatter)."

—Week Three—

Save All You Can

*Riches gotten quickly will dwindle,
    but those who acquire them gradually
    become wealthy.*
                        (Proverbs 13:11)

Jesus told the story of a master who was going on a trip and entrusted his wealth to his servants: five coins (talents) to one servant, two coins to the second, and one coin to the third, "according to that servant's ability" (Matthew 25:14-30). The first and second servants both invested their coins and doubled their value. But the third servant "dug a hole in the ground and buried his master's money." He did absolutely nothing to increase the value of the master's money.

When the master returned to settle accounts, the servants who had multiplied the value of the master's investment heard the master say, "You are a good and faithful servant! You've been faithful over a little. I'll put you in charge of much. Come, celebrate with me." When the third servant returned the coin just the way he had received it, the master called him an "evil and lazy servant." He went on, "You should have turned my money over to the bankers so that when I returned, you could give me what belonged to me with interest." (Every banker I know loves this parable!)

The master took the coin from the third servant and gave it to the first one saying, "Those who have much will receive more, and they will have more than they need. But as for those who don't have much, even the little bit they have will be taken away from them."

It's a stern parable that communicates the truth in John Wesley's instruction when he said, "Having gained all you can, by honest wisdom, and unwearied diligence, the second rule of Christian prudence is, 'Save all you can.' "[1] We can feel the strength in Wesley's conviction when we read his words:

> Do not throw the precious talent into the sea…
> Do not throw it away in idle expenses, which is
> just the same as throwing it into the sea. Expend
> no part of it merely to gratify the desire of the
> flesh, the desire of the eye, or the pride of life.[2]

Saving prudently is difficult because it calls for a radical reorganization of our lives, and that's exactly the point. It's nothing less than a conversion experience as we reorient our whole existence around the value of God's kingdom. It's in the conversion process that the power of God's spirit is released into our lives.

Wesley's rule to "save all you can" is not a justification to accumulate wealth for its own sake or to satisfy a narrow addiction to comfort and self-satisfaction. Christian disciples save all they can as a spiritual practice enabling them to grow toward a greater end—namely, discovering how our resources can be used to bring about God's kingdom on earth as it is in heaven.

Saving is a practical step along the way toward Wesley's understanding of "Christian perfection," defined as loving God with all our heart, soul, mind, and strength and loving others the way we have been loved by God. Saving is a means by which every area of our life comes under the gracious rule of God's love in Jesus Christ.

-From *Earn. Save. Give.*, by James A. Harnish

11. You Gotta Have a Plan

> *"If one of you wanted to build a tower,*
> *wouldn't you first sit down and calculate the*
> *cost, to determine whether you have enough*
> *money to complete it? Otherwise, when you*
> *have laid the foundation but couldn't finish the*
> *tower, all who see it will begin to belittle you.*
> *They will say, 'Here's the person who began*
> *construction and couldn't complete it!'"*
>
> *(Luke 14:28-30)*

Mystery lovers all have their favorite detectives. Mine are Nero Wolfe and Archie Goodwin, whose home base is a brownstone on West 35th Street in New York City. Wolfe is an overweight orchid fancier who designs elaborate meals and devours books. If he had his way he would do nothing beyond spending his daily four hours in the orchid rooms, eating the meals he designs with his personal chef Fritz, and devouring one book after another in his specially constructed chair at the desk in his office.

However, his lifestyle costs money, and that's where Archie Goodwin comes in. Archie prods and annoys Wolfe to take occasional work as a detective. Archie then expends a fair amount of shoe leather, initiative, and the occasional punch or two in seeking the facts that Wolfe needs to solve the most baffling mysteries.

Nero Wolfe and Archie Goodwin were created by author Rex Stout (1886–1975). Early in his lifetime Stout wore many hats. From 1906 to 1908, during his stint in the Navy, he worked on President Teddy Roosevelt's yacht. He spent the next four years doing over thirty different jobs in six states, all the while writing articles, short stories, and serialized novels for pulp magazines.

Stout's goal was to become a full-time writer, but there was a real-life mystery to solve: how to afford it! Odd jobs and writing for the pulps weren't providing enough. So, using what little money he had, Stout rented a hotel room to escape distractions so he could devise a way to achieve his goal and perhaps help others along the way.

The result was his ingenious invention of a school banking system. In his program, students saved money by making bank deposits through their schools. Children were taught the value of saving.

As for Rex Stout, the royalties from his program were put into savings that allowed him to write full time, which led to his creation of Nero Wolfe and Archie Goodwin.[3]

Most of us have goals for ourselves and for our churches, but how many of us sit down and think through ways to achieve those goals? It's never too early or too late to take stock of where we are and where we're going, nor to teach children and adults how to do a better job of saving and serving God.

Help us, O Lord, to make use of your gifts, and bless us with the wisdom to discern your best will for our lives. Amen.

12. Who Trusts You?

> *"His master replied, 'Excellent! You are a good and faithful servant! You've been faithful over a little. I'll put you in charge of much. Come, celebrate with me.'"*
>
> *(Matthew 25:21)*

The ancient Olympics, contrary to popular belief, were not limited to amateurs. That rule was created by the modern Olympic movement in the nineteenth century as a way of keeping out working-class people, who couldn't afford to compete without being paid.

Ancient Olympians, besides achieving fame, earned cash, houses, and sometimes even an income for life. They also brought glory to the Greek and

Roman gods, as the Olympics were a decidedly pagan event.

Enter Sarapammon, a pagan who lived during the third century, a time when Christianity was still illegal. Sarapammon was an Olympic champion. At one point he wrote a letter from Syrian Antioch to his mother, who lived in the Egyptian town of Oxyrhynchus.

> From: Sarapammon, Olympian, to his mother,
> and Didymus, many greetings!
>
> I want you to know that I am very well. I got the letter that you wrote—my brother Ion brought it—so I know all about you. Do not agonize about me. For I want you to know I am not coming home until after athletic events in Antioch, but I'll come after that. I am sending you two talents via Sotas the Christian...[4]

Two things about the letter are curious. The first is that Sarapammon was sending a very large amount of money to his mother—two talents. Jesus talked about talents in his parables, and there is some disagreement about how much a talent was worth. But one estimate is that, at the time Sarapammon's letter was written, two talents was the equivalent of forty years' salary for a common day laborer.

47

That was a staggering amount of money to save! Sarapammon couldn't transfer his money digitally, so he needed a courier he could trust. He chose a man named Sotas, whom he identifies as "the Christian." Even though Sotas was a member of an illegal religion, the pagan Olympic champion trusted Sotas the Christian to deliver a staggering sum of money to his mother.

Who was Sotas? He was the overseer or straw boss of the church at Oxyrhynchus, which meant he had a hand in the spiritual and economic life of the believers. His reputation was so good that he was trusted to deliver money to a pagan's mother![5]

Our reputation in the wider world matters, especially our reputation with regard to money. It's crucial for the church to show trustworthiness in handling the hard-earned savings of its members. How trustworthy do you consider yourself? When and how have you been trusted in the economic ministries of the church?

Divine Master, may we be found trustworthy in small and great things, in your eyes and in the eyes of the world. Amen.

13. Spare Change

> *"Or what woman, if she owns ten silver coins*
> *and loses one of them, won't light a lamp and*
> *sweep the house, searching her home care-*
> *fully until she finds it? When she finds it, she*
> *calls together her friends and neighbors, say-*
> *ing, 'Celebrate with me because I've found*
> *my lost coin.'"(Luke 15:8-9)*

Sometimes I think I'm out of step with the world. Unlike everyone I know, I enjoy receiving coins in my change. I'll fish through it, looking for National Park quarters, or Lewis and Clark nickels, or pennies commemorating the bicentennial of Lincoln's birth. Or I play the date game and try to name an important event that happened the year a coin was minted.

I've seen folks walk past pennies, nickels, dimes, and quarters that are lying on the pavement for the taking. Young people tell me they throw change in the trash. And in some cities I've seen vending machines that encourage you to bring jars full of change and turn them into dollar bills—for a price. Last time I checked, one company was charging 8.9 percent.

Now please understand, I intend no criticism of the people who invented and market these machines. More power to them! It certainly shows a clear understanding of how people feel about change.

But think about it: 8.9 percent is almost nine cents on a dollar. If you have ten bucks' worth of change, the machine gets $.89. It gets $8.90 if you dump in a hundred dollars' worth of change. There are records of folks who have brought thousands of dollars' worth of change, which can translate into hundreds of dollars for the machine.

When you think about it, that's almost a tithe! If you treated spare change with the respect it deserves, you could make a special gift to your church. In fact, why stop at 10 percent? Why not give the whole jar of coins to the church? After all, when you know the value of small things, you learn how they become big things.

Which brings us to today's Scripture. I've heard people retell Jesus' parable of the woman cleaning her house as an amusing tale or as an excuse for spring cleaning, but in ancient households the woman was often the financial manager, and she knew that one coin was a valuable asset. The fact that she had been able to save up ten coins, the equivalent of ten days' work for a day laborer, makes it clear that she knew the value of money and the importance of being a good steward.

The next time you mutter about spare change, think about the work that small sums might be doing, especially as part of our savings, where, with proper investment, they could grow into larger sums for the glory of God.

Mustard Seed God, may your inspiration grow in our hearts until, working together, we accomplish great things in your name. Amen.

14. Laura Wine's Ministry

> *Don't think to yourself, My own strength and abilities have produced all this prosperity for me. (Deuteronomy 8:17)*

Why did the Internal Revenue Service investigate Laura Wine (1899–1969) with all the resources at their command? This churchgoing school nurse spent her weekends working in an inner-city hospital on Chicago's West Side. What had she done to cause a full-blown IRS investigation of her life and work?

Perhaps it's because she put the ministry of Jesus Christ first and, because of that, saved successfully and gave sacrificially. Or perhaps it's because the

IRS couldn't bring itself to believe that anyone would give a lifelong 30 percent tithe. But that was just the way Laura Wine lived. She earned money and saved it carefully, so it was possible for her to tithe triply.

When Laura Wine was young, her dreams of becoming a missionary were dashed when she tested positive for tuberculosis. Despite her disappointment, she lived a life of service to God's people. During the week, she worked as a school nurse in the Naperville School District, in a suburb of Chicago. She spent her weekends as a nurse at the Bethany Brethren Hospital on Chicago's poorer West Side. Through it all, she saved money and put her church first, donating 30 percent of what she earned.

Upon her retirement in 1964, her health history was no longer a concern, and she fulfilled her lifelong dream of becoming a missionary. She was sent as a nurse to an underserved population in Nigeria. She worked fearlessly, despite medical dangers, until she succumbed to the first recorded case of what came to be known as Lassa Fever. Even in her death she gave back to others and to the work of the church: autopsies performed on her body helped doctors identify the disease and devise an anti-serum.

When the IRS investigated Laura Wine, all they found was a Christian who was serious about saving and giving. Her lifelong discipleship proved that she had taken today's Scripture to heart. She did not consider her hard-earned wages to be her own, and that is why she saved conscientiously and tithed triply. In today's text, God reminds the people—and us—that what seems to be ours is the result of God's goodness and that we must be good stewards, not hoarding owners, in good times and bad.[6]

I will thank you forever because of what you have done. In the presence of the faithful I will proclaim your name, for it is good. Amen.

(Based on Psalm 52:9)

15. The Last Supper Code

Pay attention, you wealthy people! Weep and moan over the miseries coming upon you.
(James 5:1)

Dan Brown's novel *The Da Vinci Code* purported to reveal secrets about Jesus that were revealed in da Vinci's painting of "The Last Supper." Never mind that the painting was produced almost fifteen hundred years after the biblical events actually took place. The fact is that art about Jesus, in da Vinci's time or ours, usually says more about us than it says about the Bible.

This fact really came home to me in an article I read in *Biblical Archaeological Review*. Brothers Craig Wansink (professor of religious studies at Virginia Wesleyan College) and Brian Wansink (professor of consumer behavior at Cornell University) examined fifty-two paintings of the Last Supper, produced over the space of a thousand years, using a computer.

What they discovered was fascinating: as food became more readily available, the size of the meal served at the Last Supper got bigger and bigger! In some ancient paintings the portions were austere, even tiny. But as times went by and perceptions of what was a "normal" portion changed, Jesus' meal grew! It was as if the apostles had stopped in the drive-through lane of a fast food place and ordered "supersized" portions.

Consider the captions from two photographs in Jared Diamond's book *The World Until Yesterday: What Can We Learn from Traditional Societies*. One caption reads, "Traditional feasting among Dani people in the Baliem Valley of the New Guinea Highlands: Traditional feasting is very infrequent, the food consumed is not fattening, and the feasters do not become obese or end up with diabetes." On the next page it says, "Modern feasting. Americans and members of other affluent modern societies 'feast' three times every day, eat fattening foods, become obese, and may end up with diabetes." [7]

It is a blessing that many of us church folks are no longer in danger of starving to death. However, we have grown to expect larger portions on our plate than we need. We complain when we are not served a feast at every meal. We are not satisfied with satisfaction. Most of us eat more than we ought, which means we spend more on food than we ought.

Think of the money we could save if we chose to buy a little less, eat a little less, and wasted a little less food. What ministries could we support more fully? What hunger programs sponsored by our church could we fund more effectively? As we consider the sacrifices Jesus made, let us consider our own sacrifices that might make a dramatic difference in the lives of others.

Dan Brown aside, maybe there really is something to be decoded in paintings of the Last Supper. If the Wansink brothers are right, the message might be "Eat less, eat better, save more, and serve God!"

God who has blessed us beyond our deserving, may we be contented with less, that we might serve you more. Amen.

WEEK THREE
ACTIVITIES

Individual

- Write an acrostic poem for *save*, about ways to reprioritize your new life in Christ.
- Establish a database to track your earning and saving.
- Pray the Beatitudes of Giving. (See the Prayer Page at the back.)
- Research median earnings in your county or community and, based on that figure, calculate a theoretical tithe. Create a church budget based on that theoretical tithe.
- List and discuss some of the ways in which TV ads encourage you to buy things you don't need.
- Select a special coin or medallion to keep in your pocket as a reminder that you don't have to spend money when you first see something you like; you can save the money instead.
- Use a calculator when you shop for groceries and determine which size and quantity of an item saves you the most money. Put the amount you save into your savings account.

Family

- Guess or find the most expensive item in your home. Then guess or find the most valued item. Discuss the difference.
- Have each family member pick one regular purchase they can go without and save the money not spent.
- Write a slogan to encourage your family to save. Create a poster designed around that slogan.
- Create on video a mock public service announcement as a family about the importance of saving. Show the video at a church event or post it online.

—WEEK FOUR—

GIVE ALL YOU CAN

Generous persons will prosper;
those who refresh others will
themselves be refreshed.
(Proverbs 11:25)

John Wesley was clear that earning and saving are not ends in themselves. They lead toward what Wesley called the "farther end" of giving.

Wesley acknowledged that when it comes to making the best use of money, "the children of this world are in their generation wiser than the children of light" (Luke 16:8 KJV), and faithful people often do not "employ it to the greatest advantage." In all his sermons on money, Wesley affirmed the importance of providing for personal and family needs. Because of his passionate engagement with the poor, he knew there was no inherent goodness in poverty. Life is better when we have what Wesley called "things needful for yourself . . . for your wife, your children, your servants, or any others who pertain to your household."[1]

Wesley was equally clear that simply earning and saving can, in fact, become an impediment to "going on to perfection" as a follower of Christ unless these practices become the means by which we move toward "a farther end," which is a life of Christ-centered generosity in which we find joy in giving all we can.

The urgency behind Wesley's sermon "The Use of Money" was his pastoral desire to lead people into a healthier, more productive, more deeply Christ-centered life by providing practical wisdom on the relationship between their faith and their finances. Wesley's rules are not about raising money for the church; they are about becoming more like Jesus. His intention was to guide the early Methodists in the spiritual discipline of generosity so they would become a giving people whose lives were shaped in the likeness of an extravagantly generous God.

The "farther end" toward which Wesley sought to move us is a life that fulfills God's best purpose for the use of our resources and equips us to participate in God's loving, saving, healing work in this world. It is a practical expression of Wesley's teaching on "Christian perfection" as the ongoing process by which the Holy Spirit continues God's work of salvation in and through us.

The "farther end" is to see the ways our money may be

> of unspeakable service...and (if we use it
> according to Christian wisdom) of doing all manner
> of good...answering the noblest ends...food for
> the hungry, drink for the thirsty, raiment for the
> naked...a defence for the oppressed, a means
> of health to the sick, of ease to them that are in
> pain; it may be as eyes to the blind, as feet to the
> lame; yea, a lifter up from the gates of death![2]

In fact, the "farther end" to which Wesley calls us is nothing less than using our money as the practical means by which we participate in God's kingdom coming on earth, even as it is already fulfilled in heaven. It's a way of embracing the love of God that walked among us in Jesus Christ and helping to ensure that that love remains a down-to-earth, human reality in this world.

-From *Earn. Save. Give.*, by James A. Harnish

16. Field of Dreams

> *There were no needy persons among them.*
> *Those who owned properties or houses would*
> *sell them, bring the proceeds from the sales,*
> *and place them in the care and under the*
> *authority of the apostles. Then it was distrib-*
> *uted to anyone who was in need.*
>
> *(Acts 4:34-35)*

Remember Sotas, the leader of the third-century Oxyrhynchus church in Egypt? The Christian who an Olympian trusted to transport a huge sum of cash to his mother? Well, six letters from the ancient world have survived that are by or about Sotas. In some ways I feel like I know him.

Thanks to these letters we know he traveled to meet with other church leaders, had a hand in preparing new Christians to be baptized, and encouraged fellow believers to support the congregation by making responsible economic choices.

That's because the early church did not put spiritual and economic matters in separate boxes, as we sometimes do. They knew all of life was connected. This is demonstrated by one of the letters, in which both spiritual and economic matters are discussed. (There are some gaps in the opening of the letter where the papyrus has holes.)

Greetings, Demetrios, holy son.
I, Sotas, greet you.

The common... is clear and our common
salvation.... For these things are provided by
God. If therefore you have decided according
to the ancient custom to give some acreage to
the [church], have it boundaried, in order that
it might be put to use, and when you decide
regarding this work let it be with confidence.
Greet everyone in your house, all of them.

I pray for the health of you all in God con-
tinuously and in everything.
[reverse side]
To my holy son Demetrios from Sotas[3]

According to Sotas, giving, receiving, praying,
and "our common salvation" are all one. There is no
separation between sacred and secular in the life of
the church. Sotas uses phrases such as "if you decide"
and "when you decide" to encourage his "holy son"
Demetrios, evidently a landowner and therefore a
person of some wealth, to donate a field thoughtfully
and "with confidence" for the use of the congregation.

And did you notice? In the third century A.D., the
decision to give money, property, and other valuables

was considered "an ancient custom." That means the church that was described in the Book of Acts hadn't disappeared. When we donate significantly to our congregation or denomination, we are part of that same ancient custom. We are part of the Acts church.

We thank you, Giving God, for the blessings we have received and for the blessings we are able to share for your work in the world. Amen.

17. Get on Board the Ark!

> *Train children in the way they should go;*
> *when they grow old, they won't depart from it.*
> *(Proverbs 22:6)*

The mission team at a congregation I served previously knew they could count on adults to support active and charitable work in the name of Jesus, both in our community and around the world. What they wondered was how to get the youngest children excited about giving and sharing with others. Then they remembered Heifer International.

Maybe you've heard of Heifer International and how its founder Dan West, while serving powdered milk to starving children during the Spanish Civil War, realized that what hungry people needed was "not a cup, but a cow." After sharing his vision with fellow farmers back in Indiana, together they developed a program that now sends animals to people around the world so they can get a new start in life.

Children love animals and love the thought of sharing animals with other people. The mission team wondered if enthusiasm about animals might help our young children get excited about the church's mission and challenge them to give money for Heifer International.

The team invited the children to figure out how they could earn enough money to make a special donation to Heifer International for what was called a "Gift Ark." Costing five thousand dollars, the donation would pay for a veritable ark of animals to be delivered worldwide.

It was decided that the children would bring spare change every other week for a special offering, and they would also pass offering plates to invite others in the church to do the same. Each week we watched these young children solemnly carry offering plates up and down the aisles. Soon everyone in the congregation began bringing spare change to put into the offering plates. Sometimes the offering plates got so heavy that two children would be needed to carry a single plate.

The education—as well as the excitement—spread through the whole church. It wasn't long before singles, fives, tens, and twenties were added to the change, along with some checks.

At first there was no set timetable to complete the offering, but then an anonymous donor offered to double whatever we raised. Suddenly the children and adults began giving even more generously, and very quickly the five thousand dollars was raised, and then it was doubled to ten thousand dollars to pay for two Gift Arks.

We made sure to celebrate and to put the children at the center of the celebration. They learned that their giving is important and that they could work to encourage others to give as well, making a real impact in the world and in the name of Jesus.

We thank you, God, for givers of all ages. May we always include each other in the great work you have set before us. Amen.

18. Do the Right Thing

> *Every good gift, every perfect gift, comes*
> *from above. These gifts come down from the*
> *Father, the creator of the heavenly lights, in*
> *whose character there is no change at all.*
>   *(James 1:17)*

My friend Karen S. Carter of Bridgewater, Virginia, wrote a book about her childhood in Nazi Germany before and during World War II. Her father was a famous composer who wrote the music for "Lili Marlene," a song beloved by both the German people and the Allies. When Karen was young, her parents divorced, and her mother reared the children in conditions of terrible privation.

The family lived in a tiny apartment during the final years of the war. Food was scarce for everyone. Karen recalled once that the cheese purchased with their ration cards turned out to have maggots: "When we complained about the little wiggly critters on our bread, Mother simply said, 'All they have eaten is cheese. So, close your eyes and eat!' And we did."

Against that background, Karen wrote about one man who had a few hens that he kept in a chicken coop. When the hens laid eggs, the man didn't share them. Then one day some of the eggs turned up missing. Who was stealing them? Infuriated, the man offered a reward of one egg to anyone who would discover the thief. Excited, Karen and her older brother devised a hiding place and kept an eye on the chicken coop. Karen was frightened about confronting the mysterious thief, but her fear was overcome by the thought of getting a delicious egg as a reward.

In spite of their efforts, Karen and her brother never discovered who was stealing the eggs. Years later, Karen told her mother how strange it was that no one had ever unmasked the thief. Her mother laughed. She revealed it was Father Manuel, the Russian Orthodox priest, who they all considered a very spiritual and holy man and who was the pastor of the man who owned the hens.

Karen's mother said that almost every night the priest would bring an egg or two that he told her to stir into the children's porridge. "They won't know it's there, but their bodies will," explained the priest. When Karen's mother objected, he said, "I know, I know, there is a commandment *Thou shalt not steal.* But in *my* faith, there is a higher one: *Thou shalt preserve life.*"[4]

In the Gospels, Jesus challenged his critics, insisting that even when a biblical law is at stake, it is important we always choose to do what is right. In our offerings we sometimes have to make difficult choices. We can't guarantee that every cent will go to the right place, nor can we guarantee that the church agencies we support will agree with us on every single issue. But regardless of the ambiguity, we must still serve God by doing the right thing and trusting that God will transform every generous act of giving.

Inspire me, Lord, by those who overcome all obstacles to see that your children are fed. Amen.

19. A Lasting Legacy

> *"Be careful that you don't practice your religion in front of people to draw their attention. If you do, you will have no reward from your Father who is in heaven."*
> *(Matthew 6:1)*

For over eleven centuries, regardless of war, famine, or economic downturn, athletes from all over the Western world came to the Olympic Games in Greece every four years to prove that they could run faster, jump higher, or lift more than anyone else. For years afterward, their exploits would be immortalized in art, sculpture, song, and poetry. The Olympics may have been even more important then than they are now.

But once, a little over a decade before the birth of Jesus, they were almost canceled. Civil wars gripped the Mediterranean region following the assassination of Julius Caesar. Athletes died in battle. Countries went bankrupt. Amid the widespread financial ruin there was serious talk of skipping the games.

However, there was a mighty king, admired for his strength, power, and astounding building projects. Indeed, he was responsible for one of the great wonders of the world, a temple on a hill, that cemented his fame. Not satisfied with that legacy, the king decided to step in and save the Olympic Games of 12 B.C. by donating huge sums so they could still be held.

In recognition of his generosity, an impressive title in his honor was created. He was declared President of the Games, a designation never used before or since. The king was pleased, assuming that his legacy would be based on his role as savior of the Olympics as well as on the building projects he left for posterity.

Not so.

The king was none other than Herod the Great,[5] who today is remembered for his cruelty, his paranoia that caused him to murder his own relatives, and, in Scripture, his wholesale slaughter of innocent children in an effort to destroy an imagined threat posed by the birth of the infant King—Jesus!

Jesus celebrated giving—for example, by the widow and by Zacchaeus—but he also warned us against giving as a means of impressing others. If we fail to live a life worthy of the salvation we have been offered, our giving does not benefit us.

Generous offerings may buy us temporary fame, but our giving will not insure us a legacy if we fail to recognize the Lordship of Christ.

Lord, all we have is yours. All we give was yours from the beginning. We are yours, Creator, Redeemer, Savior. Amen.

20. The Good Eye

> *Happy are generous people,*
> *because they give some of their food to the poor.*
> *(Proverbs 22:9)*

Have you heard of the Evil Eye? Most cultures believe in one form of it or another. It refers to the ability to affect others with a dirty look. It's an ancient belief, but even today we still say, "If looks could kill..."

Did you know there's something called the Good Eye? According to the Bible we use the Good Eye when we bless others and ourselves. It comes from the letters of Paul.

When I lived in Pennsylvania, I would drive a group of volunteers each month to Washington, D.C., to work in a soup kitchen. We would leave before dawn, arrive mid-morning, unload our food, start cooking, and find our places in the serving line. We would offer a prayer, and then it was lunch time!

We had rules to follow. There were health regulations about gloves and serving utensils and about the temperature of the water as we washed pots and pans, silverware and trays.

But we didn't need any rules when it came to smiling and welcoming the folks who arrived to eat. They got to know us, and we got to know them. They were happy to see us, and we were happy to see them. This is probably what the Apostle Paul meant when he wrote, "Each of you must give as you have made up your mind, not reluctantly or under compulsion, for God loves a cheerful giver" (2 Corinthians 9:7 NRSV).

Paul probably got that phrase, "a cheerful giver," from the ancient Greek version of today's Scripture, Proverbs 22:9. That Greek version, which he would have read as a young man, went something like this: "God blesses the one who is cheerful and also a giver" (my translation from the Greek).

The Hebrew version reads a bit differently. How do we translate it? You can read the Common English

Bible (CEB) translation at the beginning of this devotional. The New Revised Standard Version (NRSV) translates it this way:

> Those who are generous are blessed,
>> for they share their bread with the poor.

But that can also be translated as:

> Whoever has a good eye will be blessed
>> because they give from their bread
>> to the poor. (my translation)

The reason for this rather unusual alternate translation is that the words usually translated as "generous" mean literally "a Good Eye." Just as the Evil Eye was thought to cast a curse, so the Good Eye cast generosity on the poor and rebounded back in blessings to the giver.

Back in the Washington, D.C., soup kitchen, by the time we finished serving and cleaning and driving three hours, we were exhausted but also blessed. I guess that's how that Good Eye thing works.

Receive God's blessings. Be a cheerful giver.

Lord, may we receive as we have given and be blessed as we bless others, always in your name. Amen.

WEEK FOUR
ACTIVITIES

Individual

- Review the giving you do on a regular or irregular basis.
- Write an acrostic poem for *give* on how you plan to bless the work of Christ.
- Pray the Prayer of King David regarding giving. (See the Prayer Page at the back of this devotional.)
- If it's available, get a copy of your church's mission budget for the last five years.
- Pick a daily expense that you can do without, and set aside the money for the church.
- Does your congregation allow for direct deposit for purposes of tithing? Consider helping to establish such a program.
- Speak with your pastor about stewardship sermons that could be delivered by you and other members of the congregation.

Family

- Collect change at your house and offer it to a church program or project.
- Sing the hymn "Will You Let Me Be Your Servant?"
- Plan a sleepover, a jogathon, or another youth event to raise money. Seek sponsors.
- Take a census in your church of the number of coats per individual. Donate the coats you don't need.

Prayer Pages

Beatitudes of Giving

Blessed are those who sacrifice, in imitation of the sacrifice of Jesus.

Blessed are the givers, who give thanks for all they have already been given.

Blessed are those who give in kind—to them God has already kindly given.

Blessed are those who give more than lip service to peace and righteousness, who walk the walk of Jesus in every aspect of life.

Blessed are those for whom the suffering of the world is real— and who really work through offering and prayer to alleviate that suffering.

Rejoice and be glad, for God in patience has given us all another opportunity to change the world through commitment to the holy kingdom.

In our offerings today we are truly blessed. May others be blessed as well because of the opportunity we have been given in the name of Jesus.

Prayer of King David About Giving (1 Chronicles 29:10-18)

*Blessed are you, L*ORD*,*
  God of our ancestor Israel,
    forever and always.
*To you, L*ORD*, belong greatness and power,*
  honor, splendor, and majesty,
    because everything in heaven and on earth belongs to you.
*Yours, L*ORD*, is the kingship,*
  and you are honored as head of all.
You are the source of wealth and honor,
  and you rule over all.
In your hand are strength and might,
  and it is in your power to magnify and strengthen all.
And now, our God, we thank you
  and praise your glorious name.
Who am I,
  and who are my people,
    that we should be able to offer so willingly?
Since everything comes from you,
  we have given you that which comes from your own hand.
To be sure, we are like all our ancestors,
  immigrants without permanent homes.
Our days are like a shadow on the ground,
  and there's no hope.

*L*ORD*, our God, all this abundance that we have provided to build you a temple for your holy name comes from your hand and belongs to you. Since I know, my God, that you examine the mind and take delight in honesty, I have freely given all these things with the highest of motives. And now I've been delighted to see your people here offering so willingly to you.*

Lᴏʀᴅ, God of our ancestors Abraham, Isaac, and Israel, keep these thoughts in the mind of your people forever, and direct their hearts toward you.

Lord's Prayer (Matthew 6:9-13 NRSV)

Our Father in heaven,
   hallowed be your name.
Your kingdom come.
Your will be done,
   on earth as it is in heaven.
Give us this day our daily bread.
And forgive us our debts,
   as we also have forgiven our debtors.
And do not bring us to the time of trial,
   but rescue us from the evil one.

Prayer of Agur (Proverbs 30:7-9)

Two things I ask of you;
   don't keep them from me before I die:
Fraud and lies—
   keep far from me!
Don't give me either poverty or wealth;
   give me just the food I need.
   Or I'll be full and deny you,
   and say, "Who is the Lᴏʀᴅ?"
   Or I'll be poor and steal,
   and dishonor my God's name.

A Service of Commitment

Sit at a quiet place in your home, by yourself or with family members. Turn to the Prayer Pages in this devotional and read the Prayer of King David About Giving (1 Chronicles 29:10-18).

Allow a moment of silence for meditation and then, individually or as a group, write out a statement of commitment, describing what you feel God is calling you to give, in terms of money, prayer, presence, and service. Sign the statement or statements and place them in an envelope.

Then take the Pledge Card you received in the mail or at church and decide how to fill out the card. Prayerfully consider what you have learned over the previous weeks. Fill out the Pledge Card and mail or hand-carry the card to church.

Recite this litany by yourself or as a group. For individuals, recite the entire litany, using "I." For families, alternate between one and all.

One:
We have prayerfully considered our financial situation.

All:
We have prayerfully considered how to earn, save, and give all we can.

One:
In all our prayers we seek the guidance of God's wisdom, present in Scripture as well as in our own common sense that is the gift of God.

All:
Let us challenge ourselves to do more and to be more.

One:
May God's Holy Spirit guide us and guard us in this solemn and joyful endeavor to become and abide in God's wisdom, treasuring the wealth that has been entrusted to us, that the good news of Jesus Christ may be shared around the world, in our lives and in the life of our church.

All:
May our lives become a living sacrifice, in your honor, to your glory, God, Creator, Redeemer, Sustainer.

One:
Now let us pray with the words that God's Son and our Savior taught us, saying:

All:
Our Father in heaven,
    hallowed be your name.
Your kingdom come.
Your will be done,
    on earth as it is in heaven.
Give us this day our daily bread.
And forgive us our debts,
    as we also have forgiven our debtors.
And do not bring us to the time of trial,
    but rescue us from the evil one.

One:
For the kingdom, the power, and the glory are yours, now and forever.

All:
Amen!

Notes

Introduction

1. John Wesley, "The Use of Money," Sermon 50, http://www.umcmission.org/Find
-Resources/John-Wesley-Sermons/Sermon-50-The-Use-of-Money, Intro., 2, 3.

Week 1

1. Eric Hobsbawm, "Methodism and the Threat of Revolution in Britain," *History
Today*, Volume 7, Issue 5, May 1957, http://www.historytoday.com/eric-hobsbawm
/methodism-and-threat-revolution-britain.
2. John Wesley, "The Use of Money," Sermon 50, http://www.umcmission.org/Find
-Resources/John-Wesley-Sermons/Sermon-50-The-Use-of-Money, Intro., 2.
3. Frank Ramirez, "Scattered Leaves, Letters from Acculturated Christians," *Brethren Life
and Thought*, vol. 43, Winter and Spring 1998, Number 1 & 2, 72–73. *Note:* text is from
Ramirez's tranlation of the *Papyrus Amherst I (1900).*
4. Ibid.
5. Frank Ramirez, *Immersion Bible Studies: Proverbs, Ecclesiastes, Song of Solomon*
(Nashville: Abingdon Press, 2011), pp 52–55.
6. Mara Hvistendahl, "Is China's Great Wall Visible from Space?"; *Scientific American*
(February 28, 2008). http://www.scientificamerican.com/article/is-chinas-great-wall
-visible-from-space/
7. Clara Moskowitz, "AAS| Dispatch: International Borders Are Visible from Space,"
Space.com (January 14, 2012). http://www.space.com/14240-earth-international-
borders-visible-space-aas219.html.
8. Dawn Ottoni Wilhelm, *Preaching the Gospel of Mark: Proclaiming the Power of God*
(Louisville: Westminster-John Knox Press, 2008), 80–81.

Week 2

1. John Wesley, "The Use of Money," Sermon 50, http://www.umcmission.org/Find
-Resources/John-Wesley-Sermons/Sermon-50-The-Use-of-Money, Intro., 2.
2. Ibid.
3. Donald F. Durnbaugh, "Two Early Letters from Germantown"; *Pennsylvania Magazine
of History and Biography* 74 (April 1960), 219-233.
4. Ibid.

5. Ruben Vives, "California Couple's Gold Find Called Greatest in U.S. History"; *Los Angeles Times* (February 26, 2014). http://articles.latimes.com/2014/feb/26/local /la-me-ln-california-couple-gold-coin-find-20140226.

6. *Ferris Bueller's Day Off*, "Nine Times," https://www.youtube.com/watch?v=Hh _vLKlz2Mc.

7. R. Jan and Roma Jo Thompson, *Beyond Our Means: How the Brethren Service Center Dared to Embrace the World* (Elgin, IL: Brethren Press, 2009), 194–195.

8. Matthias Claudius (1782), translated by Jane M. Campbell (1861), "We Plow the Fields and Scatter," stanza 3, http://www.hymnary.org/hymn/PH1990/560.

Week 3

1. John Wesley, "The Use of Money," Sermon 50, http://www.umcmission.org/Find -Resources/John-Wesley-Sermons/Sermon-50-The-Use-of-Money, II, 1.

2. Ibid.

3. Alden Whitman, "Rex Stout, Creator of Nero Wolfe, Dead," *New York Times*, October 28, 1975, accessed March 11, 2010, http://nerowolfe.org/pdf/stout/home_family /obits/1975_10_28_NY_Times_Obit.pdf..

1. Frank Ramirez, translator. *Brief des Sarapammon an seine Familie*, A.D. 250-299, Florence, Istituto Papirologico 'G. Vitelli', http://papyri.info/ddbdp/sb;12;10772 (accessed March 3, 2015).

4. AnneMarie Luijendijk, *Greetings in the Lord: Early Christians and the Oxyrhynchus Papri* (Harvard University Press, 2009), 136–141.

5. Frank Ramirez, *Brethren Brush with Greatness* (Elgin, IL: Brethren Press, 2008), 66–71. (For more on this story see: *Fever! The Hunt for a New Killer Virus*, by John G. Fuller, Reader's Digest Press, 1974).

6. Jared Diamond, *The World Until Yesterday: What Can We Learn from Traditional Societies?* (New York: Viking Press, 2012), Plates 26–27.

Week 4

1. John Wesley, "The Use of Money," Sermon 50, http://www.umcmission.org/Find -Resources/John-Wesley-Sermons/Sermon-50-The-Use-of-Money, III, 3.

2. Ibid., Intro, 2.

3. Frank Ramirez, translator. *Papyrus Oxyrhynchus XII (1916) 1492*, late 3rd–early 4th A.A., The British Museum, London, England. *Translator's note*: Sotas does not actually write church. He used the word *place*, which was code for church.

4. Karen S. Carter, *How I Came to Be Who I Am* (CreateSpace Independent Publishing Platform, 2014), 145–147.

5. Ilan Ben Zion, "How Herod the Tyrant Saved the Olympics," *The Times of Israel* (February 7, 2014) , http://www.timesofisrael.com/how-herod-the-tyrant-saved -the-olympics/